Coloring Book For Grownups

Color Away Stress

50 Funny Fruit & Vegetable Images

By

Lamees A.

Visit http://www.colorawaystress.com

and get a free book

Visit http://www.colorawaystress.com

and learn how to color

Visit http://www.colorawaystress.com

and share your experience

Visit http://www.colorawaystress.com

and share your colored pages from the book

Feel free to email me, I would love to hear from you

Lamees@lameesauthor.com

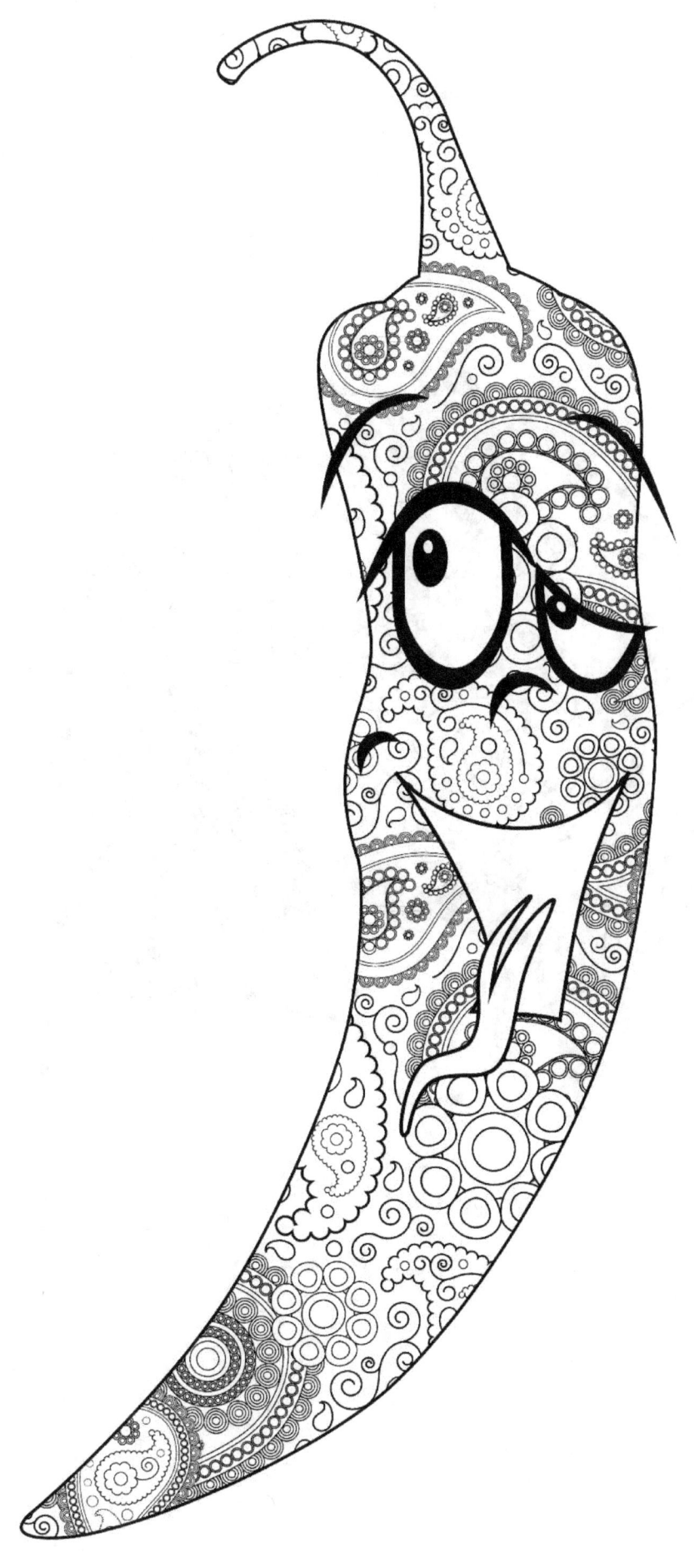

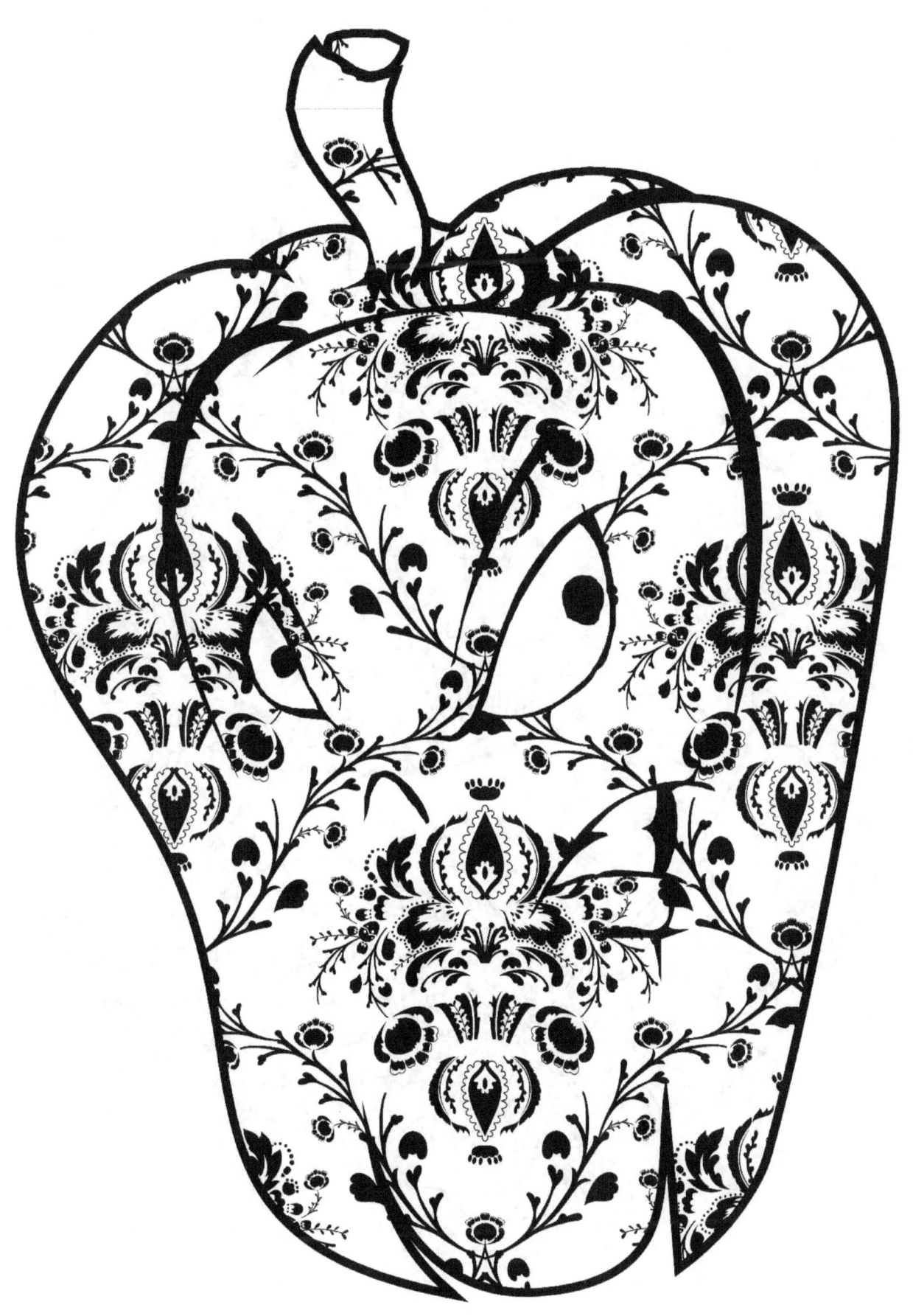

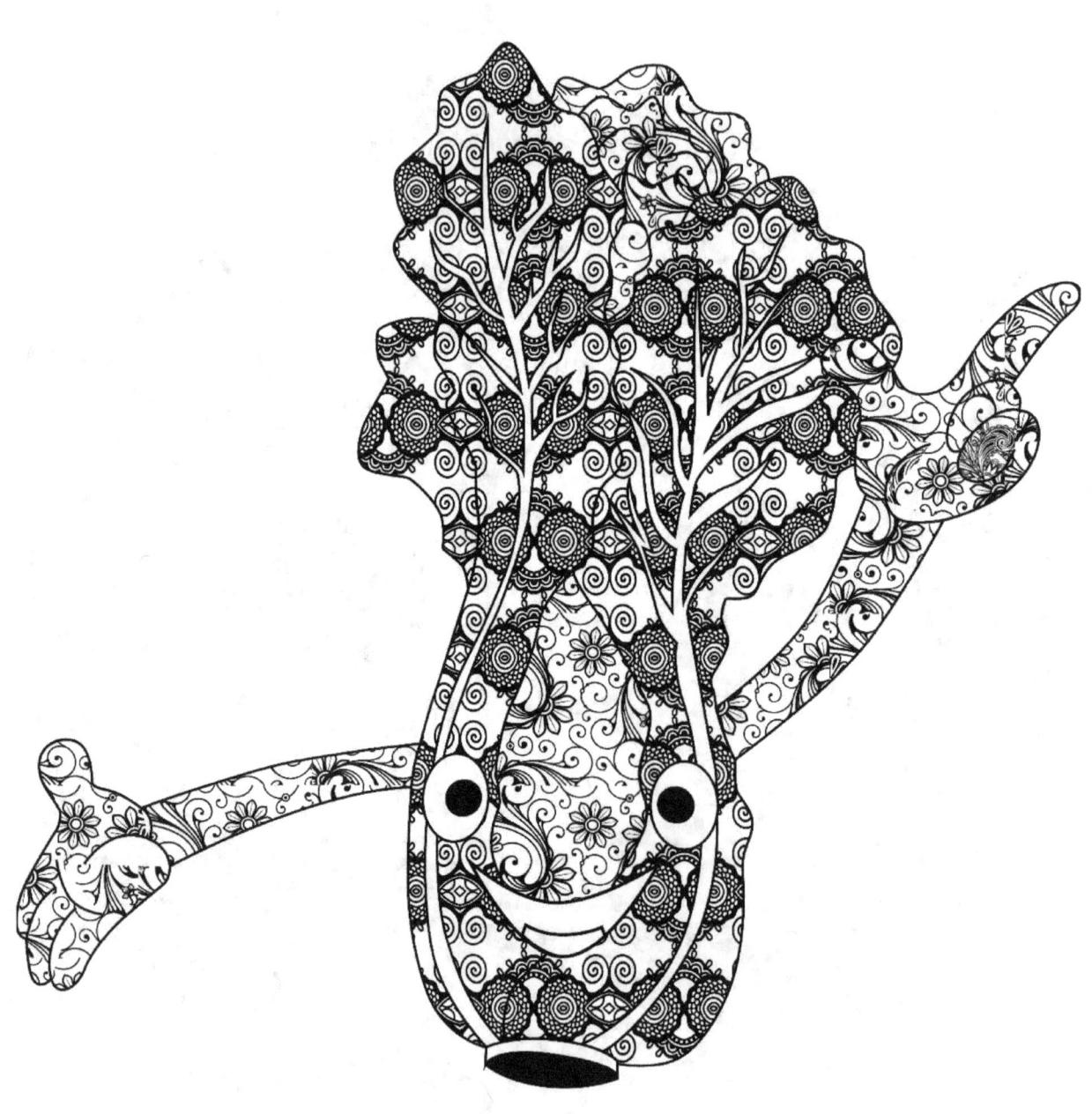

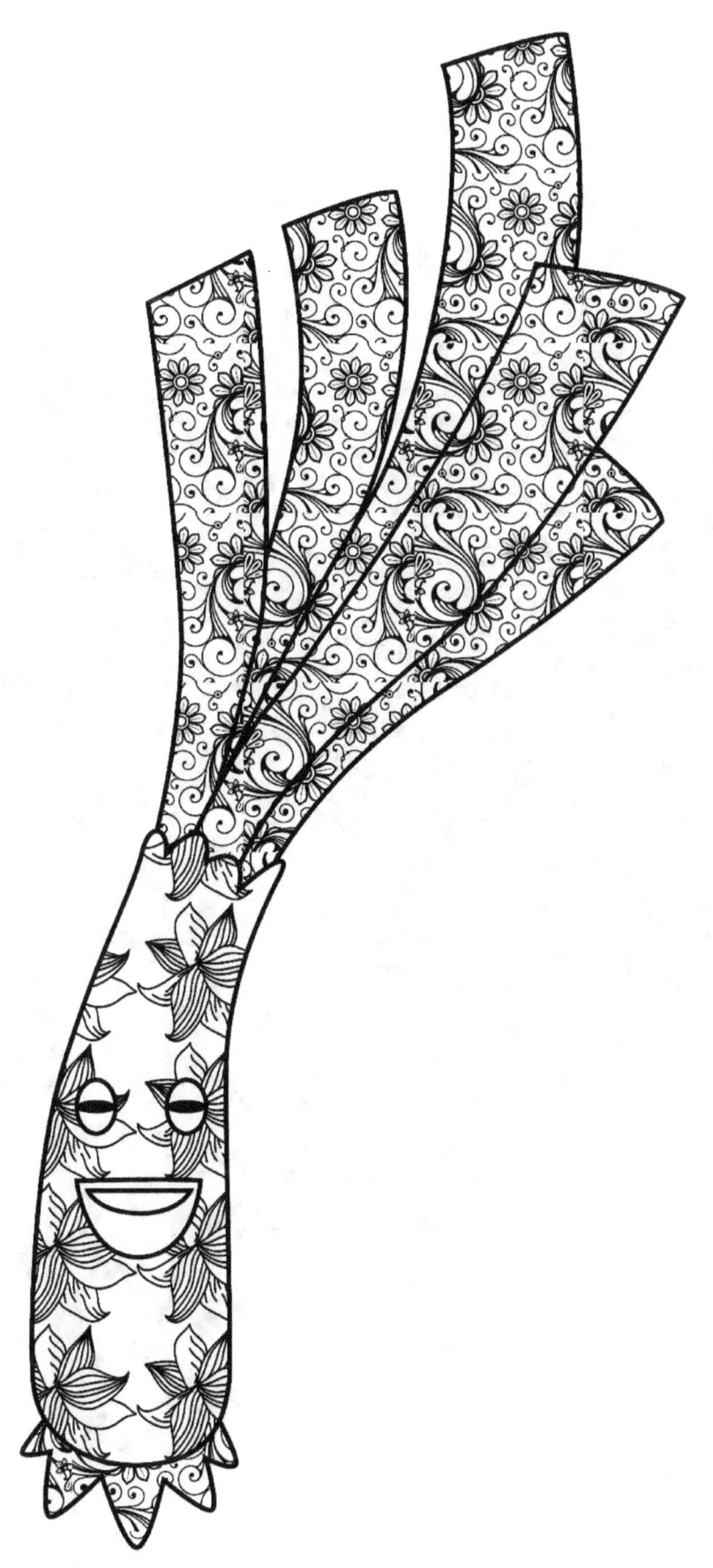

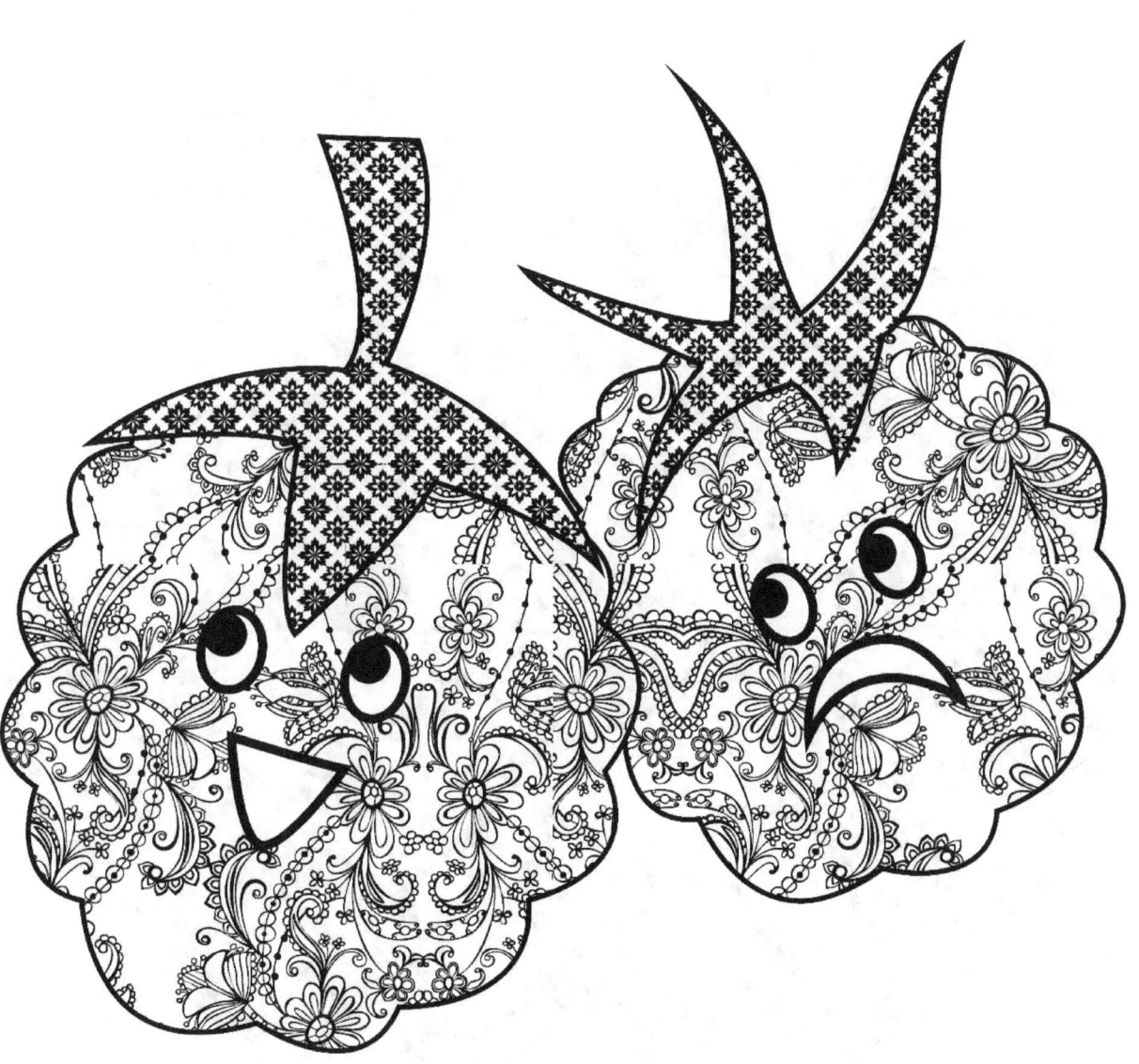

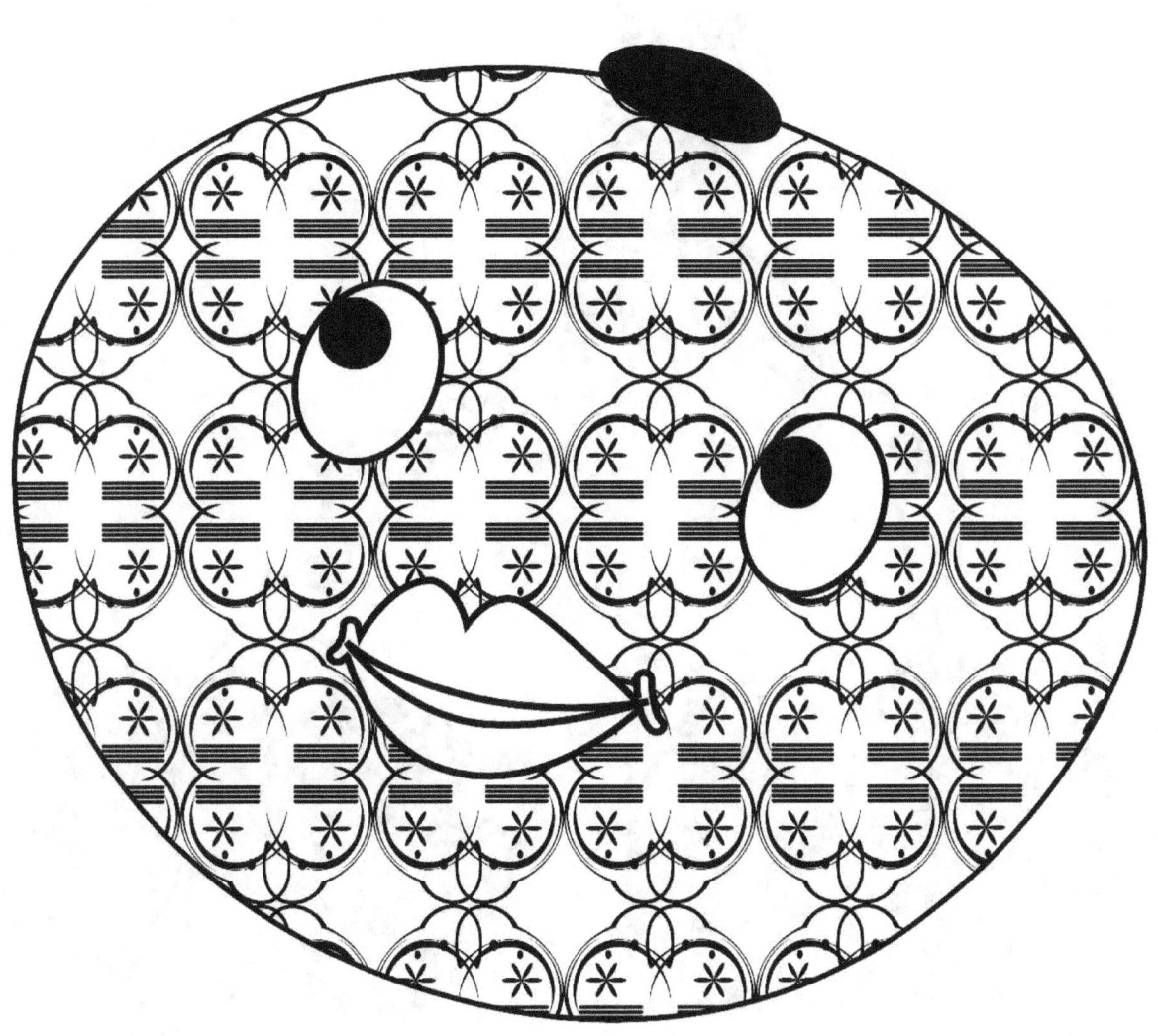

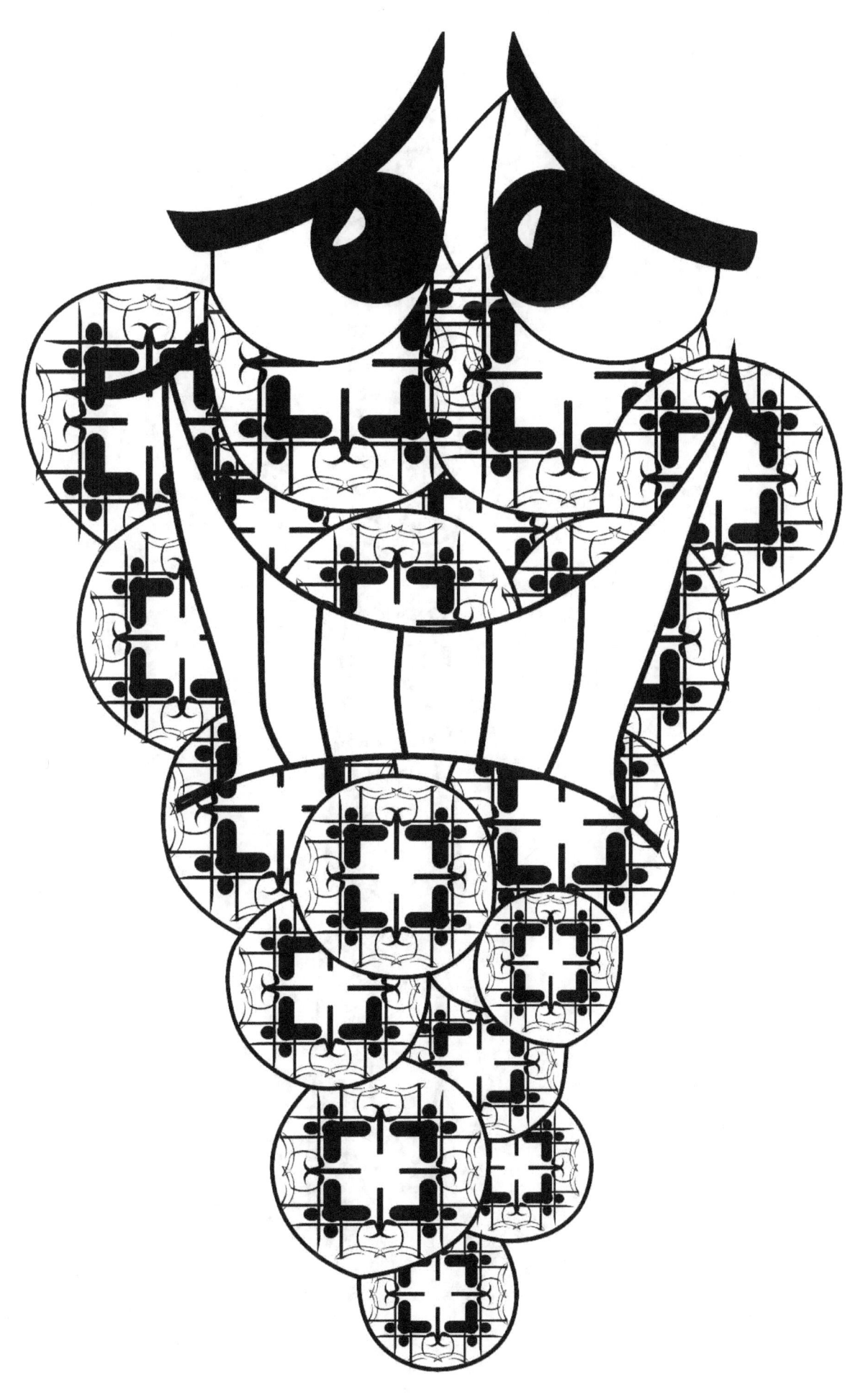

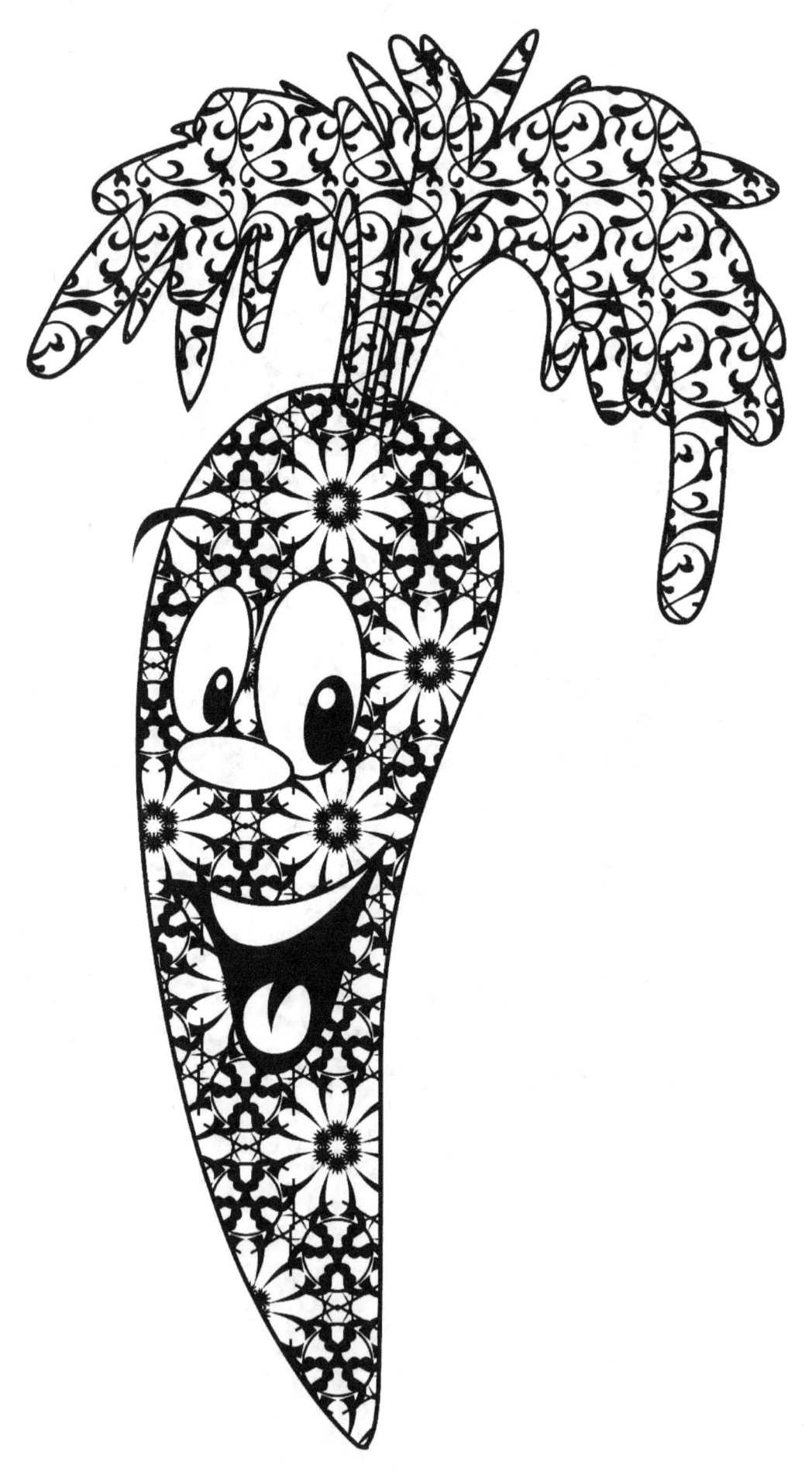